OWEN

&

SASSOON

OWEN

&

SASSOON

THE EDINBURGH POEMS

Edited by
Neil McLennan

Polygon

Published in Great Britain in 2022 by Polygon,
an imprint of Birlinn Ltd.

Birlinn Ltd
West Newington House
10 Newington Road
Edinburgh EH9 1QS

9 8 7 6 5 4 3 2 1

ISBN 978 1 84697 620 9
EBOOK ISBN 978 1 78885 555 6

British Library Cataloguing-in-Publication Data
A catalogue record for this book is available on request
from the British Library.

Typeset in Verdigris MVB by The Foundry, Edinburgh
Printed and bound in Great Britain by Clays Ltd, Elcograf S.p.A.

In Memoriam

Catherine Walker MBE, David Eastwood and Professor Douglas Weir.
Three great mentors sadly passed before this book was published.

For Poppyscotland, Royal British Legion Scotland and Forces Children
Scotland (formerly Royal Caledonian Education Trust) who, for over a
century, have cared for those who have served and serve. After reading
this collection I ask you to make a donation to
each worthy charity.

Lest We Forget

CONTENTS

PART II

THE SIEGFRIED SASSOON COLLECTION

INTRODUCTION

Combatants and observers recording their thoughts and feelings in verse was not unique to the First World War. It will, however, always be distinguished by its poets. Poems written during this period continue to be read, taught and celebrated. Fascination with the war poets, and in particular Wilfred Owen, has grown over time, especially during the 1960s after the publication of Cecil Day Lewis's *The Collected Poems of Wilfred Owen*. This edition was particularly resonant with the anti-war sentiment of the Vietnam War era. Since then, Owen and Siegfried Sassoon have become synonymous with remembrance each November. Despite the Treaty of Versailles being signed over a century ago, interest in the poets of the time continues.

Historians continue to use poetry from the war to help gain insight into the experiences of soldiers and civilians. Most people will have studied the war poets in their schooldays – the words of Owen and of Sassoon are popular and used in many classrooms. However, perhaps few will be aware that Owen and Sassoon's most powerful poems were written while in Edinburgh, Scotland's capital.

Even though they were together in the city for such a brief time, their story has been told through popular fictionalised accounts: Pat Barker's 1991 novel, and subsequent film, *Regeneration*, Stephen MacDonald's 1983 play *Not About Heroes* and most recently Terence Davies' *Benediction*. These dramatisations give us an insight into the men's time spent at

Craiglockhart War Hospital but they don't explore the effect they had on each other's work. This is the first collection to focus on the poems Owen and Sassoon wrote while in Edinburgh. They met there in the middle of August 1917 and would go on to write some of the most important poems of the war. This book pays close attention to how they influenced each other, but it also looks at other factors that played a part in their poetic development.

* * *

Wilfred Owen was injured twice on the Western Front, his second injury in April 1917 affecting him mentally as much as physically. Suffering from what was then called 'shell shock' (or 'neurasthenia' recorded in the Craiglockhart Hospital Admission and Discharge Registers) he transferred from field dressing stations to field hospitals in France, and then back to the UK for treatment and convalescence. In June 1917 he was sent to Craiglockhart War Hospital, situated near Slateford in Edinburgh. It was opened as a military hospital in 1916, one of a handful of hospitals across the country caring for 'shell-shocked' officers.

It was at this hospital that Owen met fellow officer and poet Siegfried Sassoon, a noted and decorated war hero. Sassoon's reason for being their was perhaps more complex; it was more of a political imprisonment after his criticism of the continuation of the war. His position put him at odds with the military authorities, and a medical referral to Craiglockhart (or 'Dotty-ville' as he nicknamed it) probably enabled him to avoid a court martial and its potential consequences.

On arrival at Craiglockhart, Wilfred Owen was assigned to Dr Arthur John Brock. Brock practiced innovative 'ergotherapy approaches' in part inspired by Patrick Geddes. These approaches saw activity and connections with nature take precedent over draconian military-medical 'cures' for 'shell shock'.

Meanwhile, Siegfried Sassoon was assigned to Dr William Halse Rivers Rivers. The pioneering of dream analysis and talking cures that Rivers undertook was akin to modern-day counselling. While Sassoon was perhaps not 'shell-shocked' on the surface of it, he certainly had been impacted by the war and indeed his criticism of it. Sassoon and Rivers struck up a strong bond and remained in contact for years to come. Sassoon's 'Dreamers', 'Counter-Attack' and most of his other Edinburgh poems are of course about his wartime experience. Dreams played an important part of Sassoon's doctor's thinking. Dr Rivers would go on to write *Conflict and Dreams* (1923).

The methods of Brock and Rivers continued to have an influence on the development of psychiatry in the post-war period, building on a long history of medical innovation in Edinburgh. There is now a Rivers Centre at the Royal Edinburgh Hospital in Morningside. Perhaps one day a Brock Centre may bring together his ergotherapy approaches.

* * *

My interest in war poetry was significantly piqued when I was working at Tynecastle High School in Gorgie. 'Tynie', as it is called locally, opened as a technical school in 1912. I took on the post of Head of History at the school in 2007. The school has a fascinating history that I was keen to tap into. I was interested in finding out about famous former pupils students could aspire to. I discovered that Wilfred Owen had taught at the school during his time in Edinburgh. As part of Dr Brock's ergotherapy programme of cures, some of the recovering 'shell-shocked' patients taught classes to the boys at the school as part of their recovery. The headmaster's logbook noted the arrival of officers to take classes, and Owen's letters also attest to him teaching at 'the Big School' – Tynecastle. Owen taught English Literature whilst the other officers taught map reading, physical exercise, signalling and first aid.

In researching this book, I wanted to find out where Owen was each day, who he was meeting, what he was doing and how that was influencing his writing. I also wanted to find out the effect the city, and its citizens, had on his writing. This included studying Owen's interactions with Sassoon and how much this impacted on both their creative output. This gives a new perspective to how Edinburgh and the people he met influenced his poetry.

When the two met, it was only Sassoon that was a published poet. However, Owen's time in Edinburgh saw the publication of his first poems. During his time at Craiglockhart Owen edited six issues of the hospital magazine – *The Hydra*. The publication had been set up by Dr Brock to engage patients in creative work. Owen not only edited the magazine but also had his first poems published in it. Previously it was thought that Owen had five poems published in his lifetime. However, I have found that in fact he had six. The poems were: (1) 'Song of Songs', (*The Hydra*, 1 September 1917); (2) a fragment of a poem in Owen's editorial in *The Hydra* which possibly later made up the poem 'The Dead-Beat', this fragment has previously been overlooked in reports of the poet's published work while he was alive (*The Hydra*, 1 September 1917); (3) 'The Next War', (*The Hydra*, 29 September 1917); (4) 'Miners', (*The Nation*, 26 January 1918), (5) 'Futility', (*The Nation*, 15 June 1918); (6) 'Hospital Barge', (*The Nation*, 15 June 1918). *The Nation*, which contained an eclectic range of writing, published both Owen and Sassoon. Its editors were not scared to publish work that criticised the conduct of the war. Overall, Owen's published material included the small-scale hospital magazine with a very limited circulation, alongside the widely-read national publication.

* * *

Sassoon's writing at Craiglockhart focussed more on his war experience than on pursuit of development of style. However, Owen was finding himself in many ways and developing his style as well as recovering from 'shell shock'. As such, we see him move from the Keats- and Scott-influenced 'flowery' juvenilia of his early poems such as: 'Ballad of Lady Yolande', 'Wrestlers' and 'Lines to a Beauty seen in Limehouse' to the punchier, powerful 'Dulce et Decorum Est' and 'Anthem for Doomed Youth' – poems which etched his name in history. The assistance Sassoon provided during the drafting of these poems is well documented, but there were other influences at work in 1917.

Brock's treatment of Owen by ergotherapy utilised his patient's writing as a device for downloading the trauma of war onto paper. 'The Sentry', 'The Letter', 'Inspection', 'Dulce et Decorum Est', are all examples of wartime experiences, written as part of this treatment. We see specifically his writing of the war hospital experience in 'Conscious', probably recollecting Owen's time in hospital in France, before his transfer to Edinburgh's Craiglockhart War Hospital; 'Mental Cases' is almost certainly a reflection of some of the patients far worse off than Owen in that hospital: 'Drooping tongues from jaws that slob their relish, / Baring teeth that leer like skulls' teeth wicked?' – these are men whose minds the War had ravished. 'Disabled' reflects on those injured by war whom Owen would have seen while in Edinburgh. Owen comments on the subject of the poem attending football matches 'carried shoulder-high' and having 'drunk a peg' before joining the war as 'Someone had said he'd look a god in kilts'. That changed for this young Scottish soldier as he 'sat in a wheeled chair . . . / Legless, sewn short at elbow.' 'Now, he will spend a few sick years in institutes', Owen reflected, noting the sadness of war and how the young man's pre-war popularity with the girls had turned to pity and avoidance. 'Why don't they come?' the young soldier asks, just as he too may be asking 'Dulce et decorum est pro patria mori'? reflecting on what he has been through.

* * *

Edinburgh is at the heart of many of Owen's poems. 'Dulce et Decorum Est' and 'Disabled' were written after he met Robert Graves, along with Siegfried Sassoon, at Baberton Golf Club in Edinburgh. Elsewhere, in other Owen poems, we can see Edinburgh coming through explicitly. Clearly 'Six O'clock in Princes Street' is an Edinburgh poem and was written whilst in Edinburgh. 'Who is the god of Canongate?', albeit possibly written later, between November 1917 and early 1918 in

Scarborough, has an Edinburgh setting and recalls Owen's time there. Other connections are more subtle. 'Anthem for Doomed Youth' is as much an Edinburgh poem as it is a Western Front poem. The 'Doomed Youth' (or 'Dead Youth' as it was in a first draft) may well be the boys in Owen's English Literature classes at Tynecastle High School. Furthermore, the 'cattle' so powerful an analogy in the first line, may well have been inspired by the cattle arriving at Edinburgh's meat market at Chesser, near Slateford. Owen would have passed the Slateford railway siding, the nearby field and abattoir as he walked from the war hospital to teach classes at Tynecastle. The beasts' journey to death mimicked that of the doomed generation of 1914–1918. The timing of the poem's drafting fits with the period he taught at the school.

'Schoolmistress' is also linked to Owen's teaching experience and it may be about Mrs Fullarton, the teacher at Tynecastle High School whose English classes Owen supported and with whom he built a strong friendship. Fullarton was one of a handful of Edinburgh people whom Owen wanted to be given a copy of his poems, should they ever be published. The number of Edinburgh connections on that list gives an indication of how much Owen's four-month stay in Edinburgh impacted on him personally. Sadly, Owen never saw the collection published in his lifetime. He was killed whilst crossing the Sambre Oise canal, Ors, with a week of the war left. His parents were given the news on Armistice Day as church bells rang out to celebrate the end of the war.

Another Edinburgh person whom Owen wrote a poem specifically about, or for, was Arthur Newboult, the son of family friends, who lived in Leith. 'Sweet is your antique body, not yet young' is thought to have been about Newboult for whom Owen had an affinity. There is some debate about the extent of such relationships in certain circles. Questions about Owen and Sassoon's sexuality dominate many narratives of their poems.

Owen's association with homosexuality is reflected on by one of his biographers, Dr Jane Potter. She wrote in 2014 that biographer Dominic Hibberd categorically stated that Owen was gay. However, Potter herself suggests there is no historical evidence of any sexual encounters. Professor Joseph Cohen thought there was a conspiracy of silence about Owen's homosexuality.

Although other biographers have noted Owen's interaction with the opposite sex, few have explicitly said Owen was bisexual. Having reviewed the research, and in particular biographer Jon Stallworthy's notes on Owen's trips to Milnathort in Fife, I believe it is only right we acknowledge Owen's female relationships to give some balance to understanding the man and his poems.

Stallworthy is the only biographer to write about Owen and Sassoon's trips to Milnathort. The pair visited The Thistle Inn in Minathort, a popular establishment with army officers, including those from a nearby camp. Albert Dauthieu, who ran The Thistle Inn, was an Escoffier trained chef who had worked at the Savoy in London before moving to Scotland. Stallworthy tells the story of one evening in the Inn that involved singing, joviality and perhaps romance. Stallworthy noted that Albertine Marie Dauthieu, Albert's nineteen-year-old daughter, found Owen 'charming and gay' (meaning as of the time, as opposed to today). However, Stallworthy did not disclose his findings that shared the exchanges of affection and adoration of the two young lives. It appears there was a strong connection between Owen and Dauthieu. They may have met many more times. Indeed, they wrote to each other and were at one point betrothed to each other. Although Dauthieu was already committed to a Scottish officer, a deal was struck that whoever came back from the war first would take her hand in marriage. Sadly neither man returned. Owen wrote the poem 'The Ballad of Many Thorns' which many, including Stallworthy, thought to be dedicated or about Albertine.

Another poem written for her by Owen was found in Albertine's autograph book. It is thought the poem was an adaptation of what they had sung together one night at the piano in the Inn – lines from the opera *Merrie England*. The untitled poem fragment talks of a 'Thistle' and a 'Rose'.

The reason Owen and Sassoon travelled to Milnathort, though, is unclear. Was it the easy rail links over the Forth? Was it the golf course next to the Inn which attracted Sassoon? Was it the splendid food of Albert Dauthieu? Was it the attraction of Albertine Dauthieu? Or was it just the venue providing good camaraderie for officers who visited? The golfing link seems uncanny given the earlier Baberton Golf Club meeting of Owen, Sassoon and Graves. Sassoon had also written about the hallowed ground of St Andrews in his 1916 poem 'David Cleek' and golf certainly was his prominent pleasure whilst in Scotland in 1917.

* * *

Including Owen's and Sassoon's Edinburgh poems side by side here for the first time acknowledges their poetic partnership forged in the city, and reminds us, I hope, of the mutual benefit each gained from the other.

After the war, it was Sassoon who ensured the posthumous publication of Owen's poems. Individually they are highly regarded poets, but their personal stories highlight the importance of other people and their temporary environment in inspiring and developing their work. Whilst Owen was influenced by the people whom he connected with in Edinburgh, mainly as a result of Dr Brock's innovative techniques, Sassoon used his 'stay' at Craiglockhart to visit old friends and travel. As well as travelling to Milnathort, he probably also visited St Andrews – we see from *The Hydra* that patients did play golf there. Sassoon also visited Glasgow (we know he was in the Grand Central Hotel from his letters to Lady Margaret Sackville) and he also went to North Berwick – again for golf one presumes.

Owen noted in his letters how important Edinburgh was to him. This book helps shape a better understanding of Owen's time in Edinburgh and how this impacted on his poetry. Owen and Sassoon certainly supported each other, however, the popular narrative of Sassoon as the sole and dominant influence needs to be tempered with reflections on how a wider network supported Owen's development in late 1917. After the war, Sassoon continued publishing. Owen produced his most powerful works to date in Edinburgh. 'Anthem for Doomed Youth' and 'Dulce et Decorum Est' are his best-known poems, indeed perhaps the quintessential war poems after John McCrae's 'In Flanders Fields'. Both Owen and Sassoon, through poetry, brought powerful reflections on the war to others. Their writing helped them in their own journey through the trauma of what they had experienced. Ultimately, writing brought enjoyment – a humanising sense of creativity.

Neil McLennan

PART I

THE WILFRED OWEN COLLECTION

BALLAD OF LADY YOLANDE

[fragment]

My Ladye owed a stripling lad
    Unto her privie page.
Though five and ten he scantly had,
    Both stalwarte was and sage;
And in his scarlette sylke y-clad,
    Was the flower of her equipage.

———————

His cheek was red as bin her owne
    And full as red his lips.
O he bin white as ivory bone
    Whan by the stream he strips.
His body were like the white, white stone,
    Which the cunning mason chips.

———————

His skin to her were lavender
    All bloomy after rain;
I-wis twas like my Lady's myrhh
    That charmeth her from pain.

———————

But whan she conned she was overfond,
    She sudden him dismissed.
Unto the Baron Oberond
    She sent him all unkissed.

———————

'A sign, a sign, the Baron cried,
    A lovesome sign to boot!
I ween my Ladye hath complied
    At last unto my suit!

'A token fair, the Baron sware,
    Marry, Ile wear thee well!
Fair Yolande redes me not despair,
    And right this page I spell!

'Now hie thee fast, my new page-boy,
    With greetings fair from me;
And say that I will render her joy
    Of many such child as thee.'

Dame Yolande in her bower above
    Wept sore upon her sill;
Whan lo! she spied her little boy love
    Come loping up the hill.

'O welcome to me back again!
    How come ye back so soon?'
– 'My lord he sent me back again
    With thanks for thy love boon.
Right fain is he to be thy man –'
    Well nigh did Yolande swoon.

'O haste thee, haste thee, tell him nay.
    I have another knight.
Bethink thee of some name to say,
    Some foe an if ye might,
Whom he may challenge for a fray.
    Then back and tell me light!'

Merrily ran the boy of glee,
    And knelt his lord before.
'Alas! my lord, it cannot be!
    Thy lady weepeth sore,

'And saithe, Ah me! it cannot be!
    She loves another more:
Sir Lance that is thine enemy,
    That wards the western shore.

'But thus saithe Lady Yolande,
    If e'er ye two should match,
That she will take the baron's hand
    That deadlier then shall ratch.'

He pricked away at prime of day
    Towards the western march
And soon he is come to Sir Lance the Gay,
    Was on his gateway arch.

'Ho! Gay, sly lord of Yolande
    And have I found thy earth?'
Says 'Who is this thine Yolande?'
    And gins to be in mirth.

––––––––––

'I love a jest, and love a joust
    Now which for be ye come?'
Says: 'Get thee horses and get thee housed,
    And then be frolicsome!'

––––––––––

I-wis it were not long to tell
    Of charge or shock or din;
Lord Oberon from his charger fell
    At the first closing in.

––––––––––

Then courteously Sir Lance lit down
    Nor yet drew out his brand,
But stroke his horse's neck so brown
    Till the other should upright stand.

––––––––––

He rose as might a sentinel
    That fallen hath with sleep.
Shamefast he rose, and in his selle
    All suddenly did leap.

And off he rode with spur and goad,
    With furious mein and dour;
I-wis he neither slacked or slowed
    Till he came to my Ladye's Tower;
Then up and through the hall he strode,
For alle the porter him forbode,
    And gained the Ladye's bower.

FITTE II.

Now look we unto Yolande
    A wily dame is she;
And pray her knight may lose his brande
    To Lance the enemy.

He had not ridden down the fell
    But down the fell and awaye,
When she sommon'd up her sweet angèl
    To dally with her and playe

And when he had song a lyttle tune,
    She bad him sitt and rest,
She bad him doff his running shoon
    If that they him distressed.

(For to her eyne it was a boon
　　To see his feet ondressed.)

And doff me now thy sylken vest
　　Its colour likes me not'
For she loved best to see his breast,
　　A seemlier sylke, I wot.

———————

She stood him on her falding-stool,
　　Her arms about his knees.
He let her lips so soft and cool
　　To kiss him where she please.

———————

All tremblinge stood the tender youth,
　　And gently laughed a while.
He loved her too in secret-sooth,
　　Nor now did it beguile.

———————

Then in and burst the Baron rude
　　'Gods death! What passeth here?
What shame is – By the holy rood,
　　Is this thy leman deare?'

———————

– 'Alack, she cried, my shame is oute,
　　My shame of long agone.

But now no shame am I aboute
    This is my own deare soone.

———————

His father is Sir Price the Prince,
    And this is our own sonne.
Sir Price hath ill beloved me since;
    Alas! I am undone!

———————

So well she lied to putt him offe,
    So deep was her device,
He scarce began his mail to doff,
    Whan he donned it for Sir Price.

———————

He took him sword, he took him spear,
    A trusty lance of larch,
And fully girt in fighting gear,
    Made for the wild welsh march.

And when he found Sir Prince's plas
    And quoth his quarrel just,
Said, 'let us try if they cuirass
    Be truer than thy trust,
And we see if thy heart of brass
    Withstand my lance's thrust.'

'– Thou bleatest like a drowning goat;
        What madman may ye be.
When I have smolte they silly throat
        Thou shalt not bleat so free.
When I have drowned thee in my moat
        Thou shalt not lie to me.'

Then out he shot his shining sword:
        Sir Oberond lit down;
And they fought there on the slippery sward
        That was so short and brown.

A nimble man was old Sir Price
        And leapt like any buck
And thrice he slipped and rose up thrice,
        Before the Baron struck.

Then Oberond he craved a truce
        For To lay by his mail
Him seemed it was but little use
        Free hand were more avail.

Forth then he stood withouten casque
        Withouten glove or corse.
A better target did not ask,
        Sir Price than that huge torse

[Craiglockhart, June–July 1917]

THE FATES

They watch me, those informers to the Fates
Called Fortune, Chance, Necessity, and Death;
Time, in disguise as one who serves and waits,
Eternity as girls of fragrant breath.
I know them. Men and Boys are in their pay,
And those I hold my trustiest friends may prove
Agents of Theirs to take me if I stray
From fatal ordinance. If I move, they move –

Escape? There is one unwatched way; your eyes,
O Beauty! Keep me good that secret gate!
And when the cordon tightens of the spies
Let the close iris of your eyes grow great.
So I'll evade the vice and rack of age
And miss the march of lifetime, stage by stage.

[Craiglockhart, June–July 1917]

THE WRESTLERS

[Fragment]

So neck to neck and obstinate knee to knee
Wrestled those two; and peerless Heracles
Could not prevail nor catch at any vantage;
But those huge hands which small had strangled snakes
Let slip the writhing of Antæas' wrists;
Those club of hands that wrenched the necks of bulls
Now fumbled round the slim Antæas' limbs
Baffled. Then anger swelled in Heracles,
And terribly he grappled broader arms,
And yet more firmly fixed his grasping feet,
And up his back the muscles bulged and shone
Like climbing banks and domes of towering cloud.
Many who watched that wrestling say he laughed, –
But not so loud as on Eurystheus of old,
But that his pantings, seldom loosed, long pent
Were like the sighs of lions at their meat.
Men say their fettered fury tightened hour by hour,
Until the veins rose tubrous on their brows
And froth flew thickly-shivered from both beards.
As pythons shudder, bridling-in their spite
So trembled that Antæas with held strength,
While Heracles, – the thews and cordage of his thighs
Straitened and strained beyond the utmost stretch
From quivering heel to haunch like sweating hawsers –
But only staggered backward. Then his throat

Growled, like a great beast when his meat is touched,
As if he smelt some guile behind Antæas,
And knew the buttressed bulking of his shoulders
Bore not the mass to move it one thumb's length.
But what it was so helped the man none guessed,
Save Hylas, whom the fawns had once made wise
How earth herself empowered him by her touch,
Gave him the grip and stringency of winter,
And all the ardour of the invincible spring;
How all the blood of June glutted his heart;
And the wild glow of huge autumnal storms
Stirred on his face, and flickered from his eyes;
How, too, Poseidon blessed him fatherly
With wafts of vigour from the keen sea waves,
And with the subtle coil of currents –
Strange underflows, that maddened Heracles.
And towards the night they sundered, neither thrown.
Whereat came Hylas running to his friend

While Heracles, the thews and cordage of his thighs
Straightened and strained beyond the utmost stretch,
Quivering and sweating like taut hawsers,
But only staggering backward. Then his throat
Growled, like a great beast when his meat is touched;
As if he smelt some guile behind Antæas,
And knew the bulking of his shoulders
Carried not weight buttressed to move it one thumb's length.
And towards the night they sundered, neither thrown.

Whereat came Hylas running to his friend,
With fans, and sponges in a laving-bowl,
And brimmed his lord the beakerful he loved,
Which Heracles took roughly, even from him.
Then spake that other from the place he stood:
'O Heracles, I know thy fights and labours,
What man thou wert, and what thou art become,
The lord of strength, queller of perilous monsters,
Hero of heroes, worthy immortal worship,
But me though canst not quell. For I, I come
Of Earth, and to my father Poseidon,
Whose strength ye know, and whose displeasure ye know.
Therefore be wise, and try me not again,
But say though findst me peer, and more than peer.'

But Heracles, of utter weariness,
Was loath to answer, either yea or nay.
And a cruel murmur rankled through the crowd.
Now he whose knees propped up the head of him,
Over his lord's ear swiftly whispered thus:

'If thou could'st lift the man in air – enough.
His feet suck secret virtue of the earth.
Lift him, and buckle him to thy breast, and win.'
Up sprang the son of Perseus deeply laughing
And ere the crimson of his last long clutch
Had faded from the insolent's throat, again

They closed. Then he, the Argonaut,
Remembering how he tore the oaks in Argos,
Bound both his arms about the other's loins
And with a sudden tugging, easily
Rooted him up; and crushed his inmost bones.

[Forth to the town he strode, and through the streets,
Bearing the body light as leopard-skins,
And glorious ran the shouting as he strode –

Some say his foot falls made an earthquake there
So that he dropped Antæas: some say not:
But that he cast him down by Gea's altar
And Gea sent that earthquake for her son.
To rouse him, he rose, dust
Alive, and came to Heracles
Who feasted with the people & their King.
Fain would all make high place for him any there
But he would not consent. And Hercules,
Knowing the hate of H. for his deeds,
Feasted & slept; and so the man,
And early on the morrow passed with H.
Down to the Argo, for the wind was fair.

[Craiglockhart, July 1917]

SWEET IS YOUR ANTIQUE BODY, NOT YET YOUNG

Sweet is your antique body, not yet young.
Beauty withheld from youth that looks for youth.
Fair only for your father. Dear among
Masters in art. To all men else uncouth
Save me; who know your smile comes very old,
Learnt of the happy dead that laughed with gods;
For earlier suns than ours have lent you gold,
Sly fauns and trees have given you jigs and nods.

But soon our heart, hot-beating like a bird's,
Shall slow down. Youth shall lop your hair,
And you must learn wry meanings in our words.
Your smile shall dull, because too keen aware;
And when for hopes your hand shall be uncurled,
Your eyes shall close, being opened to the world.

[Scarborough, December 1917]

SONG OF SONGS

Sing me at dawn but only with your laugh;
   Like sprightly Spring that laugheth into leaf;
   Like Love, that cannot flute for smiling at Life.

Sing to me only with your speech all day,
   As voluble leaflets do. Let viols die.
   The least word of your lips is melody.

Sing me at dusk, but only with our sigh;
   Life lifting seas it solaceth: breathe so,
   All voicelessly, the sense that no songs say.

Sing me at midnight with your murmurous heart;
   And let its moaning like a chord be heard
   Surging through you and sobbing unsubdued.

[Craiglockhart, June–August 1917]

LINES TO A BEAUTY SEEN IN LIMEHOUSE
[Fragment]

I saw you absent, watching distant lands,
Far overlooking these my lifted hands.

I saw thee sitting like a god,
That may have cared for such as barefoot trod,
And smiled calm acquiescence to their prayers
But surely sees not me I watched thy lips which I had dyed

Vermillion like a gods; so with dips
With mud own blood in dreams that woke me faint.
I saw the smooth, smooth nàked knees. Restraint
Lay heavy on them, as the fates of men
Oh gods' still knees and they were polished round, as when
A thousand asking hands have rubbed the idols.
For (So, against reverie thy knees my of old sidles.
Heavy the eyes with incense of old bridals.
I also offered sweetness but too mild
To move thee. Yet thought thy nostril smiled.
Was there no watching in those eye's aversion –
They were vacant with divine desertion –
Or were they

They lips are light vermillion,
By the brushing of a million mine own in dreams blood
Thine eyes are shuttered lest their gleams eclipse
The glory of thy hair's coronal glow.
Heavy thine eyelids, like a god's, with incense.

Thy knees are polished – with the
As are the knees of gods with many prayers
Poor incense: yet methought thy nostrils smiled.

Yet shall the city dust powder thy cheek
And Yet shall thy brows be given to a soiled pillow at night
(Thy hands shall be gloved with?)
Because you are poor
And they shall touch thy hands who neither see nor feel,
Who neither perceive nor seek perfection
And thou shalt be for ever such as gods
That look with vast inestimable eyes
Not seeing with those emeralds how men die
Because the spirit of god is far,
And takes its pleasure where no sufferings are.
So thou shall take thy pleasure far from me
Forget, or never know the image

The image wherebefore I lie and moan

Where love is easy, and no customs

And shall the dust of this foul city
Darken thy marble cheek? Fools call thee pretty,
Who art the eternal beauty my tears
Which I would wash with and tears

To night shall thy mouth's petals give their bloom
To soiled pillows in tattered room
And shall they touch thy fingers, who not feel,
Nor see, nor care for beauty: whom thy heel.
Could crush, if I might tell thee how.
But love weak because of such a thou.
The old fear of beauty chuckles now.

* * *

And thou must be fore ever a half-god,
Immortal clay, incomparable clod,
And look with vast inestimable eyes
Not seeing, with those emeralds, who dies,
Because the spirit of the god is far
Taking strange pleasures, where no weepers are,
Where love is easy, and no customs bind,
So shalt thou take thy pleasures with thy kind,
Where love is easy, where I cannot go –
What image I have, garlanded, what throne,
What sacrifice wherewith I lie and moan.

[This poem is heavily edited by Owen with some sections almost
impossible to understand in terms of sequencing. The above is a best
effort; a piecing together from photographs of the various drafts and
Jon Stallworthy's attempts at sequencing.]

[Craiglockhart, July–August 1917]

HAPPINESS

Ever again to breathe pure happiness,
So happy that we gave away our toy?
We smiled at nothings, needing no caress?
Have we not laughed too often since with Joy?
Have we not stolen too strange and sorrowful wrongs
For her hands' pardoning? The sun may cleanse,
And time, and starlight. Life will sing great songs,
And gods will show us pleasures more than men's.

Yet heaven looks smaller than the old doll's-home,
No nestling place is left in bluebell bloom,
And the wide arms of trees have lost their scope.
The former happiness is unreturning:
Boys' griefs are not so grievous as youth's yearning,
Boys have no sadness sadder than our hope.

[Revised at Craiglockhart, June–August 1917]

HAS YOUR SOUL SIPPED

Has your soul sipped
    Of the sweetness of all sweets?
Has it well supped
    But yet hungers and sweats?

I have been witness
    Of a strange sweetness,
All fancy surpassing
    Past all supposing.

Passing the rays
    Of the rubies of morning,
Or the soft rise
    Of the moon; or the meaning
Known to the rose
    Of her mystery and mourning.

Sweeter than nocturnes
    Of the wild nightingale
Or than love's nectar
    After life's gall.

Sweeter than odours
    Of living leaves,
Sweeter than ardours
    Of dying loves.

Sweeter than death
    And dreams hereafter
To one in dearth
    Of life and its laughter.

Or the proud wound
    The victor wears
Or the last end
    Of all wars.

Or the sweet murder
    After long guard
Unto the martyr
    Smiling at God;

To me was that smile,
    Faint as a wan, worn myth
Faint and exceeding small
    On a boy's murdered mouth.

Though from his throat
    The life-tide leaps
There was no threat
    On his lips.

But with bitter blood
    And the death-smell
All his life's sweetness bled
    Into a smile.

[Craiglockhart, July–August 1917]

THE DEAD-BEAT

He dropped, – more sullenly than wearily,
Lay stupid like a cod, heavy like meat,
And none of us could kick him to his feet;
– Just blinked at my revolver, blearily;
– Didn't appear to know a war was on,
Or see the blasted trench at which he stared.
'I'll do 'em in,' he whined. 'If this hand's spared,
I'll murder them, I will.'

        A low voice said,
'It's Blighty, p'raps, he sees; his pluck's all gone,
Dreaming of all the valiant, that *aren't* dead:
Bold uncles, smiling ministerially;
Maybe his brave young wife, getting her fun
In some new home, improved materially.
It's not these stiffs have crazed him; nor the Hun.'

We sent him down at last, out of the way.
Unwounded; – stout lad, too, before that strafe.
Malingering? Stretcher-bearers winked, 'Not half!'

Next day I heard the Doc's well-whiskied laugh:
'That scum you sent last night soon died. Hooray!'

[Craiglockhart, 22 August 1917]

FRAGMENT

from *The Hydra* No. 10, which may have formed
part of 'The Dead-Beat'

Who cares the Kaiser frowns imperially?
The exempted shriek at Charlie Chaplin's smirk.
The *Mirror* shows how Tommy smiles at work.
And if girls sigh, they sigh ethereally,
And wish the Push would go on less funereally.
Old Bill enlarges on his little jokes.
Punch is still grinning at the Derby blokes.
And Belloc prophecies of last year, serially.

[Craiglockhart, September 1917]

MY SHY HAND

My shy hand shades a hermitage apart, –
  O large enough for thee, and thy brief hours.
Life there is sweeter held than in God's heart,
  Stiller than in the heavens of hollow flowers.

The wine is gladder there than in gold bowls.
  And Time shall not drain thence, nor trouble spill.
Sources between my fingers feed all souls,
  Where thou mayest cool thy lips, and draw thy fill.

Five cushions hath my hand, for reveries;
  And one deep pillow for thy brow's fatigues;
Languor of June all winterlong, and ease
  For ever from the vain untravelled leagues.

Thither your years may gather in from storm,
And Love, that sleepeth there, will keep thee warm.

[Craiglockhart, August 1917]

I KNOW THE MUSIC

[Fragment]

All sounds have been as music to my listening.
Pacific lamentations of slow bells.
The crunch of boots on blue snow – rosy – glistening.
Shuffle of autumn leaves; and all farewells.

Bugles that sadden all the evening air,
And country bells clamouring their last appeals
Before music of evening prayer
Bridges, sonorous under carriage wheels.

Gurgle of sluicing surge through hollow rocks
The gluttonous lapping of the waves on weeds
Whisper of grass; the myriad-tinkling flocks.
The warbling drawl of flutes and shepherds' reeds.

The orchestral noises of October nights
Blowing symphonetic storms
Of startled clarions
Drums, rumbling and rolling thunderous and –

Thrilling of throstles in the keen, blue dawn
Bees fumbling and fuming over 'sainfoin-fields.

[Craiglockhart, August–September 1917]

ANTHEM FOR DOOMED YOUTH

What passing-bells for these who die as cattle?
   – Only the monstrous anger of the guns.
   Only the stuttering rifles' rapid rattle
Can patter out their hasty orisons.
No mockeries now for them; no prayers nor bells;
   Nor any voice of mourning save the choirs, –
The shrill, demented choirs of wailing shells;
   And bugles calling for them from sad shires.

What candles may be held to speed them all?
   Not in the hands of boys but in their eyes
Shall shine the holy glimmers of goodbyes.
   The pallor of girls' brows shall be their pall;
Their flowers the tenderness of patient minds,
And each slow dusk a drawing-down of blinds.

[Craiglockhart, September–October 1917]

SIX O'CLOCK IN PRINCES STREET

In twos and threes, they have not far to roam,
    Crowds that thread eastward, gay of eyes;
Those seek no further than their quiet home,
    Wives, walking westward, slow and wise.

Neither should I go fooling over clouds,
    Following gleams unsafe, untrue,
And tiring after beauty through star-crowds,
    Dared I go side by side with you;

Or be you in the gutter where you stand,
    Pale rain-flawed phantom of the place,
With news of all the nations in your hand,
    And all their sorrows in your face.

[Craiglockhart, August–October 1917]

THE SENTRY

We'd found an old Boche dug-out, and he knew,
And gave us hell; for shell on frantic shell
Lit full on top, but never quite burst through.
Rain, guttering down in waterfalls of slime,
Kept slush waist-high and rising hour by hour,
And choked the steps too thick with clay to climb.
What murk of air remained stand old, and sour
With fumes from whizz-bangs, and the smell of men
Who'd lived there years, and left their curse in the den,
If not their corpses . . .

                There we herded from the blast
Of whizz-bangs; but one found our door at last, –
Buffeting eyes and breath, snuffing the candles,
And thud! flump! thud! down the steep steps came thumping
And sploshing in the flood, deluging muck,
The sentry's body; then his rifle, handles
Of old Boche bombs, and mud in ruck on ruck.
We dredged it up, for dead, until he whined,
'O sir – my eyes, – I'm blind, – I'm blind, – I'm blind.'
Coaxing, I held a flame against his lids
And said if he could see the least blurred light
He was not blind; in time they'd get all right.
'I can't,' he sobbed. Eyeballs, huge-bulged like squids',
Watch my dreams still, – yet I forgot him there
In posting Next for duty, and sending a scout
To beg a stretcher somewhere, and flound'ring about
To other posts under the shrieking air.

Those other wretches, how they bled and spewed,
And one who would have drowned himself for good, –
I try not to remember these things now.
Let Dread hark back for one word only: how,
Half-listening to that sentry's moans and jumps,
And the wild chattering of his shivered teeth,
Renewed most horribly whenever crumps
Pummelled the roof and slogged the air beneath, –
Through the dense din, I say, we heard him shout
'I see your lights!' – But ours had long gone out.

[Craiglockhart, August–October 1917]

INSPECTION

'You! What d'you mean by this?' I rapped.
'You dare come on parade like this?'
'Please, sir, it's –' ''Old yer mouth,' the sergeant snapped.
'I takes 'is name, sir' – 'Please, and then dismiss.'

Some days 'confined to camp' he got,
For being 'dirty on parade'.
He told me, afterwards, the damnèd spot
Was blood, his own. 'Well, blood is dirt,' I said.

'Blood's dirt,' he laughed, looking away,
Far off to where his wound had bled
And almost merged for ever into clay.
'The world is washing out its stains,' he said.
'It doesn't like our cheeks so red:
Young blood's its great objection.
But when we're duly white-washed, being dead,
The race will bear Field Marshal God's inspection.'

[Craiglockhart, August 1917]

THE NEXT WAR

War's a joke for me and you,
While we know such dreams are true.

SIEGFRIED SASSOON

Out there, we walked quite friendly up to Death, –
    Sat down and ate beside him, cool and bland, –
    Pardoned his spilling mess-tins in our hand.
We've sniffed the green thick odour of his breath, –
Our eyes wept, but our courage didn't writhe.
    He's spat at us with bullets, and he's coughed
    Shrapnel. We chorused if he sang aloft,
We whistled while he shaved us with his scythe.

Oh, Death was never enemy of ours!
    We laughed at him, we leagued with him, old chum.
No soldier's paid to kick against His powers.
    We laughed, – knowing that better men would come,
And greater wars: when every fighter brags
He fights on Death, for lives; not men, for flags.

[Craiglockhart, September 1917]

DULCE ET DECORUM EST

Bent double, like old beggars under sacks,
Knock-kneed, coughing like hags, we cursed through sludge,
Till on the haunting flares we turned our backs
And towards our distant rest began to trudge.
Men marched asleep. Many had lost their boots
But limped on, blood-shod. All went lame; all blind;
Drunk with fatigue; deaf even to the hoots
Of tired, outstripped Five-Nines that dropped behind.

Gas! GAS! Quick, boys! – An ecstasy of fumbling,
Fitting the clumsy helmets just in time;
But someone still was yelling out and stumbling,
And flound'ring like a man in fire or lime . . .
Dim, through the misty panes and thick green light,
As under a green sea, I saw him drowning.

In all my dreams, before my helpless sight,
He plunges at me, guttering, choking, drowning.

If in smothering dreams you too could pace
Behind the wagon that we flung him in,
And watch the white eyes writhing in his face,
His hanging face, like a devil's sick of sin;
If you could hear, at every jolt, the blood
Come gargling from the froth-corrupted lungs,
Obscene as cancer, bitter as the cud

Of vile, incurable sores on innocent tongues, –
My friend, you would not tell with such high zest
To children ardent for some desperate glory,
The old Lie: Dulce et decorum est
Pro patria mori.

[Craiglockhart, October 1917]

DISABLED

He sat in a wheeled chair, waiting for dark,
And shivered in his ghastly suit of grey,
Legless, sewn short at elbow. Through the park
Voices of boys rang saddening like a hymn,
Voices of play and pleasure after day,
Till gathering sleep had mothered them from him.

* * *

About this time Town used to swing so gay
When glow-lamps budded in the light blue trees,
And girls glanced lovelier as the air grew dim, –
In the old times, before he threw away his knees.
Now he will never feel again how slim
Girls' waists are, or how warm their subtle hands.
All of them touch him like some queer disease.

* * *

There was an artist silly for his face,
For it was younger than his youth, last year.
Now, he is old; his back will never brace;
He's lost his colour very far from here,
Poured it down shell-holes till the veins ran dry,
And half his lifetime lapsed in the hot race
And leap of purple spurted from his thigh.

* * *

One time he liked a blood-smear down his leg,
After the matches, carried shoulder-high.
It was after football, when he'd drunk a peg,
He thought he'd better join. – He wonders why.
Someone had said he'd look a god in kilts,
That's why; and maybe, too, to please his Meg,
Aye, that was it, to please giddy jilts
He asked to join. He didn't have to beg;
Smiling they wrote his lie: aged nineteen years.

* * *

Germans he scarcely thought of; all their guilt,
And Austria's, did not move him. And no fears
Of Fear came yet. He thought of jewelled hilts
For daggers in plaid socks; of smart salutes;
And care of arms; and leave; and pay arrears;
Esprit de corps; and hints for young recruits.
And soon, he was drafted out with drums and cheers.

* * *

Some cheered him home, but not as crowds cheer Goal.
Only a solemn man who brought him fruits
Thanked him; and then enquired about his soul.

* * *

Now, he will spend a few sick years in institutes,
And do what things the rules consider wise,
And take whatever pity they may dole.
Tonight he noticed how the women's eyes
Passed from him to the strong men that were whole.
How cold and late it is! Why don't they come
And put him into bed? Why don't they come?

[Craiglockhart, October 1917]

WINTER SONG

The browns, the olives, and the yellows died,
And were swept up to heaven; where they glowed
Each dawn and set of sun till Christmastide.
And when the land lay pale for them, pale-snowed,
Fell back, and down the snow-drifts flamed and flowed.

From off your face, into the winds of winter,
They sun-brown and the summer-gold are blowing;
But they shall gleam again with spiritual glinter,
When paler beauty on your brows falls snowing,
And through those snows my looks shall be soft-going.

[Craiglockhart, October 1917]

THE PROMISERS

When I awoke, the glancing day looked gay;
The air said: Fare you fleetly; you will meet him!
And when the prosp'rous sun was well begun,
I heard a bird say: Sweetly you shall greet him!

The sun fell strong and bold upon my shoulder;
It hung, it clung as it were my friend's arm.
The birds fifed on before, shrill-piping pipers,
Right down to town; and there they ceased to charm.

And there I wandered till the noon came soon,
And chimed: The time is hastening with his face!
Sly twilight said: I bring him; wait till late!
But darkness harked forlorn to my lone pace.

[Craiglockhart, August–October 1917]

THE BALLAD OF MANY THORNS

A Poet stood in parley
    With Carls a-reaping corn.
Quoth one: 'I curse the Barley,
    More sharp than any thorn.'

'Although thy hand be torn,
    Ill-spoken was thy curse:
I swear thou art forsworn,
    If Thistle wound not worse.'

So groaned a footsore Climber,
    Had scaled the bristly path:
'What thorns, Sir Carl, Sir Rimer,
    Like these the Thistle hath?'

Behold a wan youth ramble
    With bleeding cheeks forlorn,
And moans: 'The wanton bramble,
    It is the keenest thorn.'

Rode by a wounded Warrior
    Deep muttering like a lion:
'Show me the flesh wound sorrier
    Than by the barb of Iron!'

Out laughed a man of folly,
    Much wine had made him thick:
'The jolly, festive Holly
    Deals oft a nasty prick.'

There hung near by a Jesus
    With crownèd head for scorn.
'Ah by His brow, who sees us,
    Was any like His thorn?'

So sighed a leprous Palmer.
    But when he thought afresh:
'Perchance His pain was calmer,
    Than this thorn in my flesh.'

Then cried the gentle Poet:
    'Not one among ye knows:
The cruelest thorn, I know it,
    For having kissed the Rose.'

[Craiglockhart, October–November 1917]

FRAGMENT

from Albertine Marie Dauthieu's autograph book, adapted from *Merrie England* (1902), written by Basil Hood, composed by Edward German.

And so I'll have my posy
Of the fairest flower that blows
Embower'd by the Thistle
And accompanied by a Rose.

[Milnathort, 1917]

FROM MY DIARY, JULY 1914

Leaves
    Murmuring by myriads in the shimmering trees.
Lives
    Wakening with wonder in the Pyrenees.
Birds
    Cheerily chirping in the early day.
Bards
    Singing of summer, scything through the hay.
Bees
    Shaking the heavy dews from bloom and frond.
Boys
    Bursting the surface of the ebony pond.
Flashes
    Of swimmers carving through the sparkling cold.
Fleshes
    Gleaming with wetness to the morning gold.
A mead
    Bordered about with warbling waterbrooks.
A maid
    Laughing the love-laugh with me; proud of looks.
The heat
    Throbbing between the upland and the peak.
Her heart
    Quivering with passion to my pressèd cheek.
Braiding
    Of floating flames across the mountain brow.
Brooding

Of stillness; and a sighing of the bough.
Stirs
 Of leaflets in the gloom; soft petal-showers;
Stars
 Expanding with the starr'd nocturnal flowers.

[Craiglockhart, October–November 1917]

SOLDIER'S DREAM

I dreamed kind Jesus fouled the big-gun gears;
And caused a permanent stoppage in all bolts;
And buckled with a smile Mausers and Colts;
And rusted every bayonet with His tears.

And there were no more bombs, of ours or Theirs,
Not even an old flint-lock, nor even a pikel.
But God was vexed and gave all power to Michael;
And when I woke he'd seen to our repairs.

[Craiglockhart, October 1917]

GREATER LOVE

Red lips are not so red
    As the stained stones kissed by the English dead.
Kindness of wooed and wooer
Seems shame to their love pure.
O Love, your eyes lose lure
    When I behold eyes blinded in my stead!

Your slender attitude
    Trembles not exquisite like limbs knife-skewed,
Rolling and rolling there
Where God seems not to care;
Till the fierce love they bear
    Cramps them in death's extreme decrepitude.

Your voice sings not so soft, –
    Though even as wind murmuring through raftered loft, –
Your dear voice is not dear,
Gentle, and evening clear,
As theirs whom none now hear,
    Now earth has stopped their piteous mouths that coughed.

Heart, you were never hot
    Nor large, nor full like hearts made great with shot;
And though your hand be pale,
Paler are all which trail
Your cross through flame and hail:
    Weep, you may weep, for you may touch them not.

[Craiglockhart, October–November 1917]

INSENSIBILITY

1

Happy are men who yet before they are killed
Can let their veins run cold.
Whom no compassion fleers
Or makes their feet
Sore on the alleys cobbled with their brothers.
The front line withers.
But they are troops who fade, not flowers,
For poets' tearful fooling:
Men, gaps for filling:
Losses, who might have fought
Longer; but no one bothers.

2

And some cease feeling
Even themselves or for themselves.
Dullness best solves
The tease and doubt of shelling,
And Chance's strange arithmetic
Comes simpler than the reckoning of their shilling.
They keep no check on armies' decimation.

3

Happy are those who lose imagination:
They have enough to carry with ammunition.
Their spirit drags no pack.
Their old wounds, save with cold, can not more ache.
Having seen all things red,
Their eyes are rid
Of the hurt of the colour of blood for ever.
And terror's first constriction over,
Their hearts remain small-drawn.
Their senses in some scorching cautery of battle
Now long since ironed,
Can laugh among the dying, unconcerned.

4

Happy the soldier home, with not a notion
How somewhere, every dawn, some men attack,
And many sighs are drained.
Happy the lad whose mind was never trained:
His days are worth forgetting more than not.
He sings along the march
Which we march taciturn, because of dusk,
The long, forlorn, relentless trend
From larger day to huger night.

5

We wise, who with a thought besmirch
Blood over all our soul,
How should we see our task
But through his blunt and lashless eyes?
Alive, he is not vital overmuch;
Dying, not mortal overmuch;
Nor sad, nor proud,
Nor curious at all.
He cannot tell
Old men's placidity from his.

6

But cursed are dullards whom no cannon stuns,
That they should be as stones.
Wretched are they, and mean
With paucity that never was simplicity.
By choice they made themselves immune
To pity and whatever moans in man
Before the last sea and the hapless stars;
Whatever mourns when many leave these shores;
Whatever shares
The eternal reciprocity of tears.

[Craiglockhart, October–November 1917 or
Scarborough, November 1917–January 1918]

APOLOGIA PRO POEMATE MEO

I, too, saw God through mud, –
    The mud that cracked on cheeks when wretches smiled.
    War brought more glory to their eyes than blood,
    And gave their laughs more glee than shakes a child.

Merry it was to laugh there –
    Where death becomes absurd and life absurder.
    For power was on us as we slashed bones bare
    Not to feel sickness or remorse of murder.

I, too, have dropped off Fear –
    Behind the barrage, dead as my platoon,
    And sailed my spirit surging light and clear
    Past the entanglement where hopes lay strewn;

And witnessed exultation –
    Faces that used to curse me, scowl for scowl,
    Shine and lift up with passion of oblation,
    Seraphic for an hour; though they were foul.

I have made fellowships –
    Untold of happy lovers in old song.
    For love is not the binding of fair lips
    With the soft silk of eyes that look and long,

By Joy, whose ribbon slips, –
    But wound with war's hard wire whose stakes are strong;
    Bound with the bandage of the arm that drips;
    Knit in the webbing of the rifle-thong.

I have perceived much beauty
    In the hoarse oaths that kept our courage straight;
    Heard music in the silentness of duty;
    Found peace where shell-storms spouted reddest spate.

Nevertheless, except you share
    With them in hell the sorrowful dark of hell,
    Whose world is but the trembling of a flare
    And heaven but as the highway for a shell,

You shall not hear their mirth:
    You shall not come to think them well content
    By any jest of mine. These men are worth
    Your tears. You are not worth their merriment.

[November–December 1917]

THE SWIFT
An Ode

When the blue has broken
    Through the pearly heat
And the grass is woken
    By our early feet,
Oh, then to be the Lark! – With all his fun
To pelt my mate with gayest kisses,
And mount to laugh away those blisses
In shaking merriment unto the sun!

When the dark is listening
    And the leaves hang still,
While the glow-worms, glistening,
    Make the keen stars thrill,
Would I might mourn to one lorn Nightingale
And be the solace of her solitude,
Speaking my doles all clear and unsubdued
And audible to her, the Nightingale.

But when eve shines lowly,
    And the light is thinned,
And the moon slides slowly
    Down the far-off wind,
Oh, then to be of all the birds the Swift!
To flit through ether, with elves winging,
Drawn up western fires, in frenzy singing,
Along the breeze to lean and poise and drift!

Fine thou art and agile,
        O thou perfect bird,
As an arrow fragile
        By an Eros whirred;
And like a cross-bow in Cupid's grasp
Thy wings are ever stretched, for striking ready;
And like young Love thou'rt frantic and unsteady,
And sure as his thine aim, and keen as Love's thy gasp.

        Strung in tautest tension
                By the lust of speed,
        And the mad contention
                Of insatiate greed,
Thou suck'st away the intoxicating air,
Trailing a wake of song in thrilling bubbles,
Till distance drowns thee. Then thy light wing doubles,
And thou art back, – nay vanished now, Oh where?

        Down in sharp declension,
                Grazing the low pool;
        Up in steep ascension
                Where the clouds blow cool;
And there thou sleepest all the luminous night,
Aloft this hurry and this hunger,
Floating with years that knew thee younger,
Without this nest to feed, this death to fight.

Airily sweeping and swinging,
        Quivering unstable,
    Like a dark butterfly clinging
        To the roof-gable,
Art thou not tired of this unceasing round?
Long'st not for rest in mead or bower?
Must lose, as spirits lose, the power
To soar again if once thou come to ground?

    Waywardly sliding and slinging,
        Speed never slacking,
    Easily, recklessly flinging,
        Twinkling and tacking;
– Oh, how we envy thee thy lovely swerves!
How covet we thy slim wings' beauty,
Nor guess what stress of need and duty
So bent thy frame to those slim faultless curves.

    Dazzlingly swooping and plunging
        Into the nest to peep,
    Dangerously leaping and lunging –
        Hark! How the younglings cheep!

O Swift! If thou art master of the air
Who taught thee! Not the joy of flying
But of thy brood: their throttles' crying
Stung thee to skill whereof men yet despair!

Desperately driving and dashing,
    Hissing and shrieking,
Breathless hurtling and lashing,
    Seeking and seeking,
What knowest thou of grace or dance or song?
Thy cry that ringeth like a lyric,
Is it indeed of joy, a panegyric?
No ecstasy is this. By love's pain it rings strong.

O that I might make me
    Pinions like to thine,
Feathers that would take me
    Whither I incline!
Yet more thy spirit's tirelessness I crave;
Yet more thy joyous fierce endurance.
If my soul flew with thy assurance,
What field, what skies to scour! What seas to brave!

[Written in 1912, revised at Craiglockhart, August 1917]

WITH AN IDENTITY DISC

If ever I had dreamed of my dead name
High in the heart of London, unsurpassed
By Time for ever, and the Fugitive, Fame,
There taking a long sanctuary at last,

I better that; and recollect with shame
How once I longed to hide it from life's heats
Under those holy cypresses, the same
That keep in shade the quiet place of Keats.

Now, rather, thank I God there is no risk
Of gravers scoring it with florid screed,
But let my death be memoried on this disc.
Wear it, sweet friend. Inscribe no date nor deed.
But let thy heart-beat kiss it night and day,
Until the name grow vague and wear away.

[March 1917, revised at Craiglockhart, August–September 1917]

MUSIC

I have been urged by earnest violins
  And drunk their mellow sorrows to the slake
Of all my sorrows and my thirsting sins.

  My heart has beaten for a brave drum's sake.
Huge chords have wrought me mighty: I have hurled

  Thuds of gods' thunder. And with old winds pondered
Over the curse of this chaotic world, –

  With low lost winds that maundered as they wandered.

I have been gay with trivial fifes that laugh;
And songs more sweet than possible things are sweet;
And gongs, and oboes. Yet I guessed not half
Life's symphony till I had made hearts beat,
And touched Love's body into trembling cries,
And blown my love's lips into laughs and sighs.

[Begun in 1916, revised at Craiglockhart,
August–November 1917]

THE CITY LIGHTS ALONG THE WATERSIDE

The city lights along the waterside
Kindled serene as blessèd candleshine.
The fires of western heaven, far and wide,
Rose like the reredos of a mighty shrine.
Slow swung the odorous trees from side to side,
Like censers, twining twilight mist for fume;
And on the mountain, that high altar-tomb,
The sun stood full of wine, blood-sanctified.

Soft, soft as angels mounting starry stairs
The smoke upclomb to space; the while a wind
Sung like an organ voicing many prayers.
I, sliding beads, mine errors to rescind,
Of slowly slipping tears, heard God, who cares,
Ineffable God give pardon that I sinned.

[Craiglockhart, October–November 1917 or
Scarborough, November 1917–January 1918]

AUTUMNAL

If it be very strange and sorrowful
To scent the first night-frost in autumntide;
If on the moaning eve when Summer died
Men shuddered, awed to hear her burial;
And if the dissolution of one rose
(Whereof the future holds unnumbered store)
Engender human tears, – ah! how much more
Sorrows and suffers he whose sense foreknows
The weakening and the withering of a love,
The dying of a love that had been dear!
Who feels upon a hand, but late love-warm,
A hardness of indifference, live a glove;
And in the dead calm of a voice may hear
The menace of a drear and mighty storm.

[Revised at Craiglockhart, October–November 1917]

PERVERSITY

We all love more the Passed and the To Be
Than actual time, and far things more than near.
Perverse we all are somehow; calling dear
Rather the rare than fair. But as for me,
How singular and sad that I should see
More loveliness in Grecian marbles clear
Than modern flesh, to beauty insincere;
Less glory in a man than any tree.

I fall in love with children, elfin fair;
Portraits; dark ladies in dark tales antique;
Or instantaneous faces passed in streets.
I know the dim old gods that never were,
Better than men. One friend I love unique.
But now, thou canst nor dream I love thee, Keats!

[Revised at Craiglockhart, October–November 1917, or
at Scarborough, November 1917–January 1918]

THE PERIL OF LOVE

As men who call on spirits get response
And woo successfully the coy Unseen,
Deeming the thing amusement for the nonce,
But later, when dark spirits intervene
Uncalled, perceive how an invading mind,
Not to be shaken off, compels them serve
Mad promptings; poisons love of life and kind;
Drains force; clogs brain; and flusters nerve:

So I, lightly addressing me to love,
Have found too late love's grave significance.
A fierce infatuation, far above
The zeal for fame or fortune, like a trance,
Exhausts my faculties. I am a prey
Of impulse, the marasmus of decay.

[Revised at Craiglockhart, October–November 1917, or
at Scarborough, November 1917–January 1918]

THE POET IN PAIN

Some men sing songs of Pain and scarcely guess
Their import, for they never knew her stress.
And there be other souls that ever lie
Begnawed by seven devils, silent. Aye,
Whose hearts have wept out blood, who not once spake
Of tears. If therefore my remorseless ache
Be needful to proof-test upon my flesh
The thoughts I think, and, in words bleeding-fresh
Teach me for speechless sufferers to plain,
I would not quench it. Rather be my part
To write of health with shaking hands, bone-pale,
Of pleasure, having hell in every vein,
Than chant of care from out a careless heart,
To music of the world's eternal wail.

[Revised at Craiglockhart, October–November 1917, or
at Scarborough, November 1917–January 1918]

THE END

After the blast of lightning from the east,

   The flourish of loud clouds, the Chariot Throne;
After the drums of time have rolled and ceased,

   And by the bronze west long retreat is blown,
Shall Life renew these bodies? Of a truth,

   All death will he annul, all tears assuage?
Or fill these void veins full again with youth,

   And wash, with an immortal water, age?

When I do ask white Age, he saith not so:

   'My head hangs weighed with snow.'
And when I hearken to the Earth, she saith:

   'My fiery heart shrinks, aching. It is death.
Mine ancient scars shall not be glorified,
Nor my titanic tears, the seas, be dried.'

[Craiglockhart, October–November 1917]

SCHOOLMISTRESS

Having, with bold Horatius, stamped her feet
And waved a final swashing arabesque
O'er the brave days of old, she ceased to bleat,
Slapped her Macaulay back upon the desk,
Resumed her calm gaze and her lofty seat.

There, while she heard the classic lines repeat,
Once more the teacher's face clenched stern;
For through the window, looking on the street,
Three soldiers hailed her. She made no return.
One was called 'Orace whom she would not greet.

[Scarborough, January–March 1918]

MENTAL CASES

Who are these? Why sit they here in twilight?
Wherefore rock they, purgatorial shadows,
Drooping tongues from jaws that slob their relish,
Baring teeth that leer like skulls' teeth wicked?
Stroke on stroke of pain, – but what slow panic,
Gouged these chasms round their fretted sockets?
Ever from their hair and through their hands' palms
Misery swelters. Surely we have perished
Sleeping and walk hell; but who these hellish?

– These are men whose minds the Dead have ravished.
Memory fingers in their hair of murders,
Multitudinous murders they once witnessed.
Wading sloughs of flesh these helpless wander,
Treading blood from lungs that had loved laughter.
Always they must see these things and hear them,
Batter of guns and shatter of flying muscles,
Carnage incomparable, and human squander
Rucked too thick for these men's extrication.

Therefore still their eyeballs shrink tormented
Back into their brains, because on their sense
Sunlight seems a blood-smear, night comes blood-black;
Dawn breaks open like a wound that bleeds afresh.
– Thus their heads wear this hilarious, hideous,
Awful falseness of set-smiling corpses.
– Thus their hands are plucking at each other;
Picking at the rope-knouts of their scourging;
Snatching after us who smote them, brother,
Pawing us who dealt them war and madness.

[Scarborough, May–July 1918]

THE CHANCES

I 'mind as how the night before that show
Us five got talkin'; we was in the know.
'Ah well,' says Jimmy, and he's seen some scrappin',
'There ain't no more than five things as can happen, –
You get knocked out; else wounded, bad or cushy;
Scuppered; or nowt except you're feelin' mushy.'

One of us got the knock-out, blown to chops;
One lad was hurt, like, losin' both his props;
And one – to use the word of hypocrites –
Had the misfortune to be took by Fritz.
Now me, I wasn't scratched, praise God Almighty,
Though next time please I'll thank Him for a blighty.
But poor old Jim, he's livin' and he's not;
He reckoned he'd five chances, and he had:
He's wounded, killed, and pris'ner, all the lot,
The flamin' lot all rolled in one. Jim's mad.

[Craiglockhart, August–September 1917]

S.I.W.

> I will to the King,
> And offer him consolation in his trouble,
> For that man there has set his teeth to die,
> And being one that hates obedience,
> Discipline, and orderliness of life,
> I cannot mourn him.
>
> W.B. YEATS

1. The Prologue

Patting goodbye, doubtless they told the lad
He'd always show the Hun a brave man's face;
Father would sooner him dead than in disgrace, –
Was proud to see him going, aye, and glad.
Perhaps his mother whimpered how she'd fret
Until he got a nice safe wound to nurse.
Sisters would wish girls too could shoot, charge, curse . . .
Brothers – would send his favourite cigarette.
Each week, month after month, they wrote the same,
Thinking him sheltered in some Y. M. Hut,
Because he said so, writing on his butt
Where once an hour a bullet missed its aim.
And misses teased the hunger of his brain.
His eyes grew old with wincing, and his hand
Reckless with ague. Courage leaked, as sand
From the best sandbags after years of rain.
But never leave, wound, fever, trench-foot, shock,
Untrapped the wretch. And death seemed still withheld
For torture of lying machinally shelled,

At the pleasure of this world's Powers who'd run amok.

He'd seen men shoot their hands, on night patrol.
Their people never knew. Yet they were vile.
'Death sooner than dishonour, that's the style!'
So Father said.

      11. The Action
One dawn, our wire patrol
Carried him. This time, Death had not missed.
We could do nothing but wipe his bleeding cough.
Could it be accident? – Rifles go off
Not sniped? No. (Later they found the English ball.)

      111. The Poem
It was the reasoned crisis of his soul
Against more days of inescapable thrall,
Against infrangibly wired and blind trench wall
Curtained with fire, roofed in with creeping fire,
Slow grazing fire, that would not burn him whole
But kept him for death's promises and scoff,
And life's half-promising, and both their riling.

      iv. The Epilogue
With him they buried the muzzle his teeth had kissed,
And truthfully wrote the mother, 'Tim died smiling.'

[Craiglockhart, September 1917]

- 72 -

WHO IS THE GOD OF CANONGATE?

Who is the god of Canongate?
    I, for I trifle with men and fate.

Art thou high in the heart of London?
    Yea, for I do what is done and undone.

What is thy throne, thou barefoot god?
    All pavements where my feet have trod.

Where is thy shrine, then, little god?
    Up secret stairs men mount unshod.

Say what libation such men fill?
    There lift their lusts and let them spill.

Why do you smell of the moss in Arden?
    If I told you, Sir, your look would harden.

What are you called, I ask your pardon?
    I am called the Flower of Covent Garden.

What shall I pay for you, lily-lad?
    Not all the gold King Solomon had.

How can I buy you, London Flower?
    Buy me for ever, but not for an hour.

When shall I pay you, Violet Eyes?
    With laughter first, and after with sighs.

But you will fade, my delicate bud?
    No, there is too much sap in my blood.

Will you not shrink in my shut room?
    No, there I'll break into fullest bloom.

[Scarborough, November 1917–February 1918]

PART II

THE SIEGFRIED SASSOON COLLECTION

DREAMERS

Soldiers are citizens of death's grey land,
  Drawing no dividend from time's tomorrows.
In the great hour of destiny they stand,
  Each with his feuds, and jealousies, and sorrows.
Soldiers are sworn to action; they must win
  Some flaming, fatal climax with their lives.
Soldiers are dreamers; when the guns begin
  They think of firelit homes, clean beds and wives.

I see them in foul dug-outs, gnawed by rats,
  And in the ruined trenches, lashed with rain,
Dreaming of things they did with balls and bats,
  And mocked by hopeless longing to regain
Bank-holidays, and picture shows, and spats,
  And going to the office in the train.

[Craiglockhart, 1917]

EDITORIAL IMPRESSIONS

He seemed so certain 'all was going well',
As he discussed the glorious time he'd had
While visiting the trenches.
             'One can tell
You've gathered big impressions!' grinned the lad
Who'd been severely wounded in the back
In some wiped-out impossible Attack.
'Impressions? Yes, most vivid! I am writing
A little book called *Europe on the Rack*,
Based on notes made while witnessing the fighting.
I hope I've caught the feeling of 'the Line',
And the amazing spirit of the troops.
By Jove, those flying-chaps of ours are fine!
I watched one daring beggar looping loops,
Soaring and diving like some bird of prey.
And through it all I felt that splendour shine
Which makes us win.'
             The soldier sipped his wine.
'Ah, yes, but it's the Press that leads the way!'

[Craiglockhart, 1917]

WIRERS

'Pass it along, the wiring party's going out' –
And yawning sentries mumble, 'Wirers going out.'
Unravelling; twisting; hammering stakes with muffled thud,
They toil with stealthy haste and anger in their blood.

The Bosche sends up a flare. Black forms stand rigid there,
Stock-still like posts; then darkness, and the clumsy ghosts
Stride hither and thither, whispering, tripped by clutching snare
Of snags and tangles.
              Ghastly dawn with vaporous coasts
Gleams desolate along the sky, night's misery ended.

Young Hughes was badly hit; I heard him carried away,
Moaning at every lurch; no doubt he'll die to-day.
But *we* can say the front-line wire's been safely mended.

[Craiglockhart, 1917]

DOES IT MATTER?

Does it matter? – losing your legs? . . .
For people will always be kind,
And you need not show that you mind
When others come in after hunting
To gobble their muffins and eggs.

Does it matter? – losing your sight? . . .
There's such splendid work for the blind;
And people will always be kind,
As you sit on the terrace remembering
And turning your face to the light.

Do they matter? – those dreams from the pit? . . .
You can drink and forget and be glad,
And people won't say that you're mad;
For they'll know that you've fought for your country
And no one will worry a bit.

[Craiglockhart, 1917]

HOW TO DIE

Dark clouds are smouldering into red
　　While down the craters morning burns.
The dying soldier shifts his head
　　To watch the glory that returns;
He lifts his fingers toward the skies
　　Where holy brightness breaks in flame;
Radiance reflected in his eyes,
　　And on his lips a whispered name.

You'd think, to hear some people talk,
　　That lads go west with sobs and curses,
And sullen faces white as chalk,
　　Hankering for wreaths and tombs and hearses.
But they've been taught the way to do it
　　Like Christian soldiers; not with haste
And shuddering groans; but passing through it
　　With due regard for decent taste.

[Craiglockhart, 1917]

THE FATHERS

Snug at the club two fathers sat,
Gross, goggle-eyed, and full of chat.
One of them said: 'My eldest lad
Writes cheery letters from Bagdad.
But Arthur's getting all the fun
At Arras with his nine-inch gun.'

'Yes,' wheezed the other, 'that's the luck!
My boy's quite broken-hearted, stuck
In England training all this year.
Still, if there's truth in what we hear,
The Huns intend to ask for more
    Before they bolt across the Rhine.'
I watched them toddle through the door –
    Those impotent old friends of mine.

[Craiglockhart, 1917]

SICK LEAVE

When I'm asleep, dreaming and lulled and warm, –
They come, the homeless ones, the noiseless dead.
While the dim charging breakers of the storm
Bellow and drone and rumble overhead,
Out of the gloom they gather about my bed.
   They whisper to my heart; their thoughts are mine.
    'Why are you here with all your watches ended?
   From Ypres to Frise we sought you in the Line.'
In bitter safety I awake, unfriended;
And while the dawn begins with slashing rain
I think of the Battalion in the mud.
'When are you going out to them again?
Are they not still your brothers through our blood?'

[Craiglockhart, 1917]

ATTACK

At dawn the ridge emerges massed and dun
In wild purple of the glow'ring sun,
Smouldering through spouts of drifting smoke that shroud
The menacing scarred slope; and, one by one,
Tanks creep and topple forward to the wire.
The barrage roars and lifts. Then, clumsily bowed
With bombs and guns and shovels and battle-gear,
Men jostle and climb to meet the bristling fire.
Lines of grey, muttering faces, masked with fear,
They leave their trenches, going over the top,
While time ticks blank and busy on their wrists,
And hope, with furtive eyes and grappling fists,
Flounders in mud. O Jesus, make it stop!

[Craiglockhart, 1917]

FIGHT TO A FINISH

The boys came back. Bands played and flags were flying,
  And Yellow-Pressmen thronged the sunlit street
To cheer the soldiers who'd refrained from dying,
  And hear the music of returning feet.
'Of all the thrills and ardours War has brought,
This moment is the finest.' (So they thought.)

Snapping their bayonets on to charge the mob,
  Grim Fusiliers broke ranks with glint of steel,
At last the boys had found a cushy job.

                    * * *

  I heard the Yellow-Pressmen grunt and squeal;
And with my trusty bombers turned and went
To clear those Junkers out of Parliament.

[Craiglockhart, 1917]

SURVIVORS

No doubt they'll soon get well; the shock and strain
    Have caused their stammering, disconnected talk.
Of course they're 'longing to go out again,' –
    These boys with old, scared faces, learning to walk.
They'll soon forget their haunted nights; their cowed
    Subjection to the ghosts of friends who died, –
Their dreams that drip with murder; and they'll be proud
    Of glorious war that shatter'd all their pride . . .
Men who went out to battle, grim and glad;
Children, with eyes that hate you, broken and mad.

[Craiglockhart, 1917]

THE INVESTITURE

God with a Roll of Honour in His hand
Sits welcoming the heroes who have died,
While sorrowless angels ranked on either side
Stand easy in Elysium's meadow-land.
Then *you* come shyly through the garden gate,
Wearing a blood-soaked bandage on your head;
And God says something kind because you're dead,
And homesick, discontented with your fate.

If I were there we'd snowball Death with skulls;
Or ride away to hunt in Devil's Wood
With ghosts of puppies that we walked of old.
But you're alone; and solitude annuls
Our earthly jokes; and strangely wise and good
You roam forlorn along the streets of gold.

[Craiglockhart, 1917]

THRUSHES

Tossed on the glittering air they soar and skim,
Whose voices make the emptiness of light
A windy palace. Quavering from the brim
Of dawn, and bold with song at edge of night,
They clutch their leafy pinnacles and sing
Scornful of man, and from his toils aloof
Whose heart's a haunted woodland whispering;
Whose thoughts return on tempest-baffled wing;
Who hears the cry of God in everything,
And storms the gate of nothingness for proof.

[Craiglockhart, 1917]

GLORY OF WOMEN

You love us when we're heroes, home on leave,
Or wounded in a mentionable place.
You worship decorations; you believe
That chivalry redeems the war's disgrace.
You make us shells. You listen with delight,
By tales of dirt and danger fondly thrilled.
You crown our distant ardours while we fight,
And mourn our laurelled memories when we're killed.
You can't believe that British troops 'retire'
When hell's last horror breaks them, and they run,
Trampling the terrible corpses – blind with blood.

   O German mother dreaming by the fire,
While you are knitting socks to send your son
His face is trodden deeper in the mud.

[Craiglockhart, 1917]

THEIR FRAILTY

He's got a Blighty wound. He's safe; and then
    War's fine and bold and bright.
She can forget the doomed and prisoned men
    Who agonize and fight.

He's back in France. She loathes the listless strain
    And peril of his plight,
Beseeching Heaven to send him home again,
    She prays for peace each night.

Husbands and sons and lovers; everywhere
    They die; War bleeds us white.
Mothers and wives and sweethearts, – they don't care
    So long as He's all right.

[Craiglockhart, 1917]

BREAK OF DAY

There seemed a smell of autumn in the air
At the bleak end of night; he shivered there
In a dank, musty dug-out where he lay,
Legs wrapped in sandbags, – lumps of chalk and clay
Spattering his face. Dry-mouthed, he thought, 'Today
We start the damned attack; and, Lord knows why,
Zero's at nine; how bloody if I'm done in
Under the freedom of that morning sky!'
And then he coughed and dozed, cursing the din.

Was it the ghost of autumn in that smell
Of underground, or God's blank heart grown kind,
That sent a happy dream to him in hell? –
Where men are crushed like clods, and crawl to find
Some crater for their wretchedness; who lie
In outcast immolation, doomed to die
Far from clean things or any hope of cheer,
Cowed anger in their eyes, till darkness brims
And roars into their heads, and they can hear
Old childish talk, and tags of foolish hymns.

He sniffs the chilly air; (his dreaming starts),
He's riding in a dusty Sussex lane
In quiet September; slowly night departs;
And he's a living soul, absolved from pain.
Beyond the brambled fences where he goes
Are glimmering fields with harvest piled in sheaves,
And tree-tops dark against the stars grown pale;

Then, clear and shrill, a distant farm-cock crows;
And there's a wall of mist along the vale
Where willows shake their watery-sounding leaves,
He gazes on it all, and scarce believes
That earth is telling its old peaceful tale;
He thanks the blessed world that he was born . . .
Then, far away, a lonely note of the horn.

They're drawing the Big Wood! Unlatch the gate,
And set Golumpus going on the grass:
He knows the corner where it's best to wait
And hear the crashing woodland chorus pass;
The corner where old foxes make their track
To the Long Spinney; that's the place to be.
The bracken shakes below an ivied tree,
And then a cub looks out; and 'Tally-o-back!'
He bawls, and swings his thong with volleying crack, –
All the clean thrill of autumn in his blood,
And hunting surging through him like a flood
In joyous welcome from the untroubled past;
While the war drifts away, forgotten at last.

Now a red, sleepy sun above the rim
Of twilight stares along the quiet weald,
And the kind, simple country shines revealed
In solitudes of peace, no longer dim.

The old horse lifts his face and thanks the light,
Then stretches down his head to crop the green.
All things that he has loved are in his sight;
The places where his happiness has been
Are in his eyes, his heart, and they are good.

* * *

Hark! there's the horn: they're drawing the Big Wood.

[Craiglockhart, 1917]

PRELUDE: THE TROOPS

Dim, gradual thinning of the shapeless gloom
Shudders to drizzling daybreak that reveals
Disconsolate men who stamp their sodden boots
And turn dulled, sunken faces to the sky
Haggard and hopeless. They, who have beaten down
The stale despair of night, must now renew
Their desolation in the truce of dawn,
Murdering the livid hours that grope for peace.

Yet these who cling to life with stubborn hands,
Can grin through storms of death and find a gap
In the clawed, cruel tangles of his defence.
They march from safety, and the bird-sung joy
Of grass-green thickets, to the land where all
Is ruin, and nothing blossoms but the sky
That hastens over them where they endure
Sad, smoking, flat horizons, reeking woods,
And foundered trench-lines volleying doom for doom.

O my brave brown companions, when your souls
Flock silently away, and the eyeless dead
Shame the wild beast of battle on the ridge,
Death will stand grieving in that field of war
Since your unvanquished hardihood is spent.
And through some mooned Valhalla there will pass
Battalions and battalions, scarred from hell;
The unreturning army that was youth;
The legions who have suffered and are dust.

[Craiglockhart, 1917]

COUNTER-ATTACK

We'd gained our first objective hours before
While dawn broke like a face with blinking eyes,
Pallid, unshaved and thirsty, blind with smoke.
Things seemed all right at first. We held their line,
With bombers posted, Lewis guns well placed,
And clink of shovels deepening the shallow trench.
   The place was rotten with dead; green clumsy legs
   High-booted, sprawled and grovelled along the saps
   And trunks, face downward, in the sucking mud,
   Wallowed like trodden sand-bags loosely filled;
   And naked sodden buttocks, mats of hair,
   Bulged, clotted heads slept in the plastering slime.
   And then the rain began, – the jolly old rain!

A yawning soldier knelt against the bank,
Staring across the morning blear with fog;
He wondered when the Allemands would get busy;
And then, of course, they started with five-nines
Traversing, sure as fate, and never a dud.
Mute in the clamour of shells he watched them burst
Spouting dark earth and wire with gusts from hell,
While posturing giants dissolved in drifts of smoke.
He crouched and flinched, dizzy with galloping fear,
Sick for escape, – loathing the strangled horror
And butchered, frantic gestures of the dead.

An officer came blundering down the trench:
'Stand-to and man the fire step!' On he went . . .
Gasping and bawling, 'Fire-step . . . counter-attack!'
Then the haze lifted. Bombing on the right
Down the old sap: machine-guns on the left;
And stumbling figures looming out in front.
'O Christ, they're coming at us!' Bullets spat,
And he remembered his rifle . . . rapid fire . . .
And started blazing wildly . . . then a bang
Crumpled and spun him sideways, knocked him out
To grunt and wriggle: none heeded him; he choked
And fought the flapping veils of smothering gloom,
Lost in a blurred confusion of yells and groans . . .
Down, and down, and down, he sank and drowned,
Bleeding to death. The counter-attack had failed.

[Craiglockhart, 1917] (from a July 1916 draft)

TWELVE MONTHS AFTER

Hullo! here's my platoon, the lot I had last year.
'The war'll be over soon.'

        'What 'opes?'

           'No bloody fear!'

Then, 'Number Seven, 'shun! All present and correct.'
They're standing in the sun, impassive and erect.
Young Gibson with his grin; and Morgan, tired and white;
Jordan, who's out to win a D.C.M. some night;
And Hughes that's keen on wiring; and Davies ('79),
Who always must be firing at the Bosche front line.

* * *

'Old soldiers never die; they simply fide a-why!'
That's what they used to sing along the roads last spring;
That's what they used to say before the push began;
That's where they are today, knocked over to a man.

[Craiglockhart, 1917]

BANISHMENT

I am banished from the patient men who fight.
They smote my heart to pity, built my pride.
Shoulder to aching shoulder, side by side,
They trudged away from life's broad wealds of light.
Their wrongs were mine; and ever in my sight
They went arrayed in honour. But they died, –
Not one by one: and mutinous I cried
To those who sent them out into the night.

The darkness tells how vainly I have striven
To free them from the pit where they must dwell
In outcast gloom convulsed and jagged and riven
By grappling guns. Love drove me to rebel.
Love drives me back to grope with them through hell;
And in their tortured eyes I stand forgiven.

[Craiglockhart, 1917]

AUTUMN

October's bellowing anger breaks and cleaves
The bronzed battalions of the stricken wood
In whose lament I hear a voice that grieves
For battle's fruitless harvest, and the feud
Of outraged men. Their lives are like the leaves
Scattered in flocks of ruin, tossed and blown
Along the westering furnace flaring red.
O martyred youth and manhood overthrown,
The burden of your wrongs is on my head.

[Craiglockhart, 1917]

ACKNOWLEDGEMENTS

With thanks to Edward Crossan, my editor at Polygon, for persevering with me on this important and timely publication which we first plotted some years ago; the late and much missed Catherine Walker MBE, Curator of the War Poets Collection, Edinburgh Napier University and good, good friend, collaborator and research partner in all things 'war poets'. This book is in her memory and that of my other two great mentors, now sadly passed, David Eastwood and Professor Douglas Weir.

Also thanks to Lizzie MacGregor, editor and formerly Assistant Librarian at the Scottish Poetry Library who has been a staunch supporter of my work in this area and was again a great supporter when doing final edits to this important collection. My thanks also goes to Dr Jane Potter, trustee of Wilfred Owen estate; Deb Fisher and David Gray, Siegfried Sassoon Fellowship; Meg Crane, Wilfred Owen Association journal editor; Aaron Michael Lisec, archivist Southern Illinois University, Carbondale; Elizabeth Garver, Jean Cannon (formerly UTA) and the team at Harry Ransom Centre, University of Texas, Austin; Sue Usher and library staff at University of Oxford Bodleian and Weston Libraries and everyone involved in the truly magnificent resource that is The First World War Poetry Digital Archive; staff at Edinburgh Napier University Craiglockhart Library and the War Poets Collection; librarians, archivists and staff at National Library of Scotland, City of Edinburgh

Libraries, University of Edinburgh Library and Strathclyde University Library; Christine Nimmo (formerly Craiglockhart Library) for her dedicated transcribing of Admission and Discharge Registers – an important resource; Jeanne Marie-Dineur and Monsieur Mayor Jacky Duminy of Ors; former Edinburgh Lord Provost the Rt. Hon. Eric Milligan and former Lord Provost, the Rt. Hon. Frank Ross. For their academic and personal support: Professor Douglas Weir, Professor Alan Alexander, Professor Hew Strachan and Professor Yvonne McEwan. Thanks to Alan Walker, MBE, husband of the late Catherine Walker MBE – Alan helped trace the Dauthieu family which helped with some of the research in this book. Professor Hazel Hutchison, Professor Tom Weber, Mr David Eastwood; and for her support throughout this project and personal and administrative help, Mrs S. McLennan. Thanks to William Kroelinger for sharing his poetry collection as part of our 1917 events.

Finally, my thanks to all the Wilfred Owen's Edinburgh 1917–2017 Committee and supporters. Together we marked the war poets' time in Edinburgh with a significant number of events which I am sure the war poets would be proud to have known about. I hope they, and you, are proud that *their* Edinburgh work is now in print in this new collection. It is another literary link for the UNESCO City of Literature.

INDEX OF TITLES